FastTrack
MUSIC INSTRUCTION

For C Diatonic Harmonica

Harmonica 2

INTRODUCTION

Why did you buy this book, too?

You bought it because you had a great time learning to play with **Book 1**, and you can't wait to get started with more hints, tips, and tricks to make yourself the complete harp player!

We assume you've read **FastTrack® Harmonica 1**, and have worked endlessly through the many examples in that book. Having done this, you're ready to move on and so are we.

This book picks up right where **Book 1** ended. You'll learn many more exciting techniques and some of the theory that underpins all music, but don't worry—we won't bore you with unnecessary technical waffle! And, of course, the last sections of all the **FastTrack®** books are the same so that you and your friends can form a band and jam together.

So, if you're ready, finish your pizza, put the cat outside, take the phone off the hook, and let's jam!

Always remember the three Ps: **patience**, **practice**, and **pace yourself**.

We'll add one more to this list: **pride** for a job well done.

ABOUT THE AUDIO

We're glad you noticed the added bonus—audio! Each music example in the book is included on the audio, so you can hear how it sounds and play along when you're ready. Take a listen whenever you see this symbol:

Many audio examples are preceded by a one-measure "countoff" to indicate the tempo and meter. As you become more confident, try playing along with the rest of the band.

PLAYBACK+
Speed • Pitch • Balance • Loop

To access audio visit:
www.halleonard.com/mylibrary

Enter Code
7796-5662-1644-8265

Harmonica consultant: Peter Wheat

HAL•LEONARD®
CORPORATION
7777 W. BLUEMOUND RD. P.O. BOX 13819 MILWAUKEE, WI 53213

Visit Hal Leonard online at
www.halleonard.com

A QUICK REMINDER

Before we get started on the fun new stuff, let's recap what you've learned from **Book 1**.

Holding the harp!

In **Book 1**, we introduced the C method for holding the harp. Later in this book we'll discuss other methods, but for the time being, this is the one you need to know:

 Make a "C" with your left hand.

 Insert the harmonica as shown, holding it firmly but comfortably.

3 Keep your fingers arched slightly. This will allow you to control the sound better.

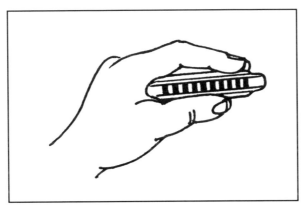

Your right hand should cup, or cradle, your left hand, with the fingers coming up around your left-hand pinky to form a seal.

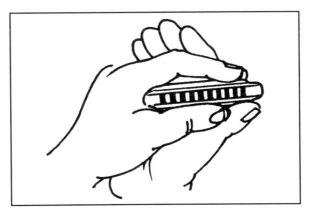

Note diagrams

In this book we'll use square box diagrams like the one below to show the layout of notes on the harmonica. For example, here are the basic blow and draw notes on a C harmonica:

Blow	C	E	G	C	E	G	C	E	G	C
Hole	1	2	3	4	5	6	7	8	9	10
Draw	D	G	B	D	F	A	B	D	F	A

Harmonica legend

When writing out harmonica music, we use a combination of traditional music notation and unique harmonica symbols. Here's a reminder of the key symbols to look out for:

1 – 10	means	**Which hole to play**
↑	means	**Blow (exhale)**
↓	means	**Draw (inhale)**
↗	means	**Half-step blow bend**
↘	means	**Half-step draw bend**
↗	means	**Whole-step blow bend**
↘	means	**Whole-step draw bend**
↘	means	**Step-and-a-half draw bend**
→	means	**Overblow**
←	means	**Overdraw**
+	means	**Push button in (chromatic harp)**

There isn't enough space here to repeat all the information on music notation from **Book 1**, but if you find anything in this book that you don't understand, check back to pages 6–7 in **Book 1**, where you'll find all the important information about reading music.

Your harmonica

The exercises in the first half of this book can all be played on a C diatonic harmonica. We introduce harmonicas in different keys in Lesson 4, so if you want to progress right through to the end of the book, you may need to invest in another couple of instruments. Don't worry, though: they're very inexpensive, and having a range of harmonicas will allow you to play many more songs and riffs, as well as make it easier for you to play with other musicians.

LESSON 1
Let's get the blues!

In **Book 1** you learned lots of familiar melodies, but in this book we're going to progress toward some more famous harmonica styles. The wail of a blues harmonica is one of the most recognizable sounds in popular music, and it's one that will earn you serious cool points.

We're going to use a lot of the techniques and tricks that you learned in **Book 1**, together with some new ideas that we'll introduce throughout the book.

Blues wailin'

Let's start with a simple single-note blues riff.

◆1 Basic Blues

3↑ 4↑ 3↓ 2↓   3↑ 4↑ 3↓ 2↓   3↑ 4↑ 3↓ 2↓   3↑ 4↑ 3↓   2↓

This is a relatively easy riff to play because you only have to move between holes that are next to each other. Notice that the first note and the last note of the riff are in fact the same note (G), but played in two different ways, either as a *blow* on the 3rd hole or a *draw* on the 2nd hole.

Concentrate on hitting each note cleanly and in time. Listen to **Track 1** to hear the phrasing, and try to emulate this as you play—this is a classic blues phrase.

SWING NOTATION, PART 1

Listen carefully to **Track 1** and compare it to the notation. Do you notice anything odd about the rhythm of the example? Well, back in Lesson 4 of **Book 1** you learned about eighth notes, which are formed by dividing a quarter note in half.

"Basic Blues" uses eighth notes, but if you listen carefully you'll hear that they're not exactly even. The first note of each pair of eighth notes is longer than the second one, giving that distinctive "chugging" blues sound. In fact, each beat is divided into three (instead of two), so the underlying pulse can be counted like this:

1 2 3, **2** 2 3, **3** 2 3, **4** 2 3

This type of rhythm is known as "swing," and eighth notes played in this way are known as "swung" eighth notes. There are other, more complicated ways of writing this down, but because this is such a common rhythm in blues, this simpler method is often used. Look for the word "swing" written at the top of a tune, which tells you to play all the eighth notes with this distinctive rhythm.

Now let's add one more note to our blues riff.

② Triplet Blues

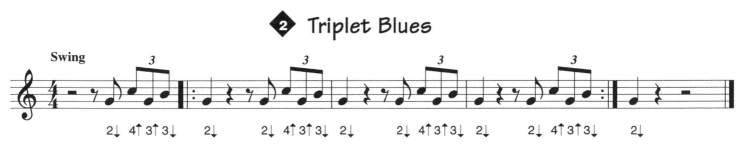

Note that this time there is a jump between the first two notes—from a draw on the 2nd hole to a blow on the 4th. Keep the tempo steady and slow—listen to the backing track and really *feel* the slow blues pulse.

SWING NOTATION, PART 2

Now that we've added an extra note to this blues riff, you see a grouping of three notes with a small "3" written over the top.

This type of rhythm is known as a **triplet**, and it is often found in tunes that are swung. This rhythmic grouping tells you to play three even notes in one beat. Remember that in swing notation, each beat is subdivided into three, not two, so one complete bar could be filled with triplets.

Try tapping your hand or foot along in time to **Track 2** and see how natural and easy it feels to tap in groups of three. Put an **accent** on the first note of each group and you'll start to get the feel of an authentic slow blues.

Bring back the bend

Back in Lesson 5 of **Book 1** you learned how to bend (lower) notes on the harmonica. It's a classic blues sound, so now we'll incorporate a bend into the riff you've just learned. Try playing "Black Cat Bend." This is just like "Basic Blues," but this time, you'll bend the third note (B) a half step as marked, making it B♭.

③ Black Cat Bend

If you're finding it difficult to get the bend on hole 3, try beginning the note with a "t" sound. This helps the bend start quicker.

In fact, there are three different draw bends available on hole 3:

Hole	3
Draw	B
1st bend	B♭/A♯
2nd bend	A
3rd bend	A♭/G♯

Each note is a half step lower than the previous one. See if you can get these different notes. Try making the mouth shape for the words "tee," "too," and "taw," and notice how the tongue moves gradually farther back in the mouth. This is not easy! It will take you some time to master each of these bends.

Some advice on bending

A lot of people find it very hard to play their first bend—don't worry if you can't do it straight away. Here are a couple of simple hints and tips that should speed things up:

1. Start with hole 4—people often find it easiest to bend using this hole.

2. Imagine saying "oy," but concentrate on what your tongue is doing and ignore your lips. It's this movement of the tongue that will enable you to bend the note.

3. Use an electronic **tuner** as you practice bending. If you see the tuner dip or change between notes, remember the feeling of your mouth and see if you can replicate it.

4. Remember to use the "t" **articulation**—this will make it easier to bend the note. It may feel a bit strange to make consonant sounds like "t" as you are breathing inwards, but persevere—it will make it easier!

Slide up, slide down

Let's expand this blues riff further by adding a slide to the front of the riff. Back in Lesson 6 of **Book 1**, you learned how to slide up to a note or chord. Guess what—you can also slide down. The key to success is knowing exactly where you want to start and finish the slide. In this case, the slide will start at hole 4 and end at hole 2. Let's practice this in the following example, "Slidin' Down."

4 Slidin' Down

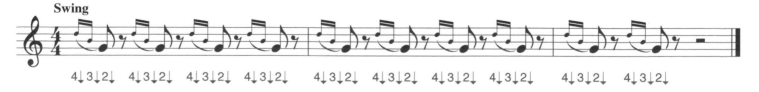

4↓3↓2↓ 4↓3↓2↓ 4↓3↓2↓ 4↓3↓2↓   4↓3↓2↓ 4↓3↓2↓ 4↓3↓2↓ 4↓3↓2↓   4↓3↓2↓ 4↓3↓2↓

This is a quick slide, so try to hit the first note cleanly and then slide down quickly to hole 2. Most harmonica teachers will tell you to try to move the harmonica and not your head. This is pretty good advice, as the harmonica is a lot lighter than your head; but if you watch harmonica players in real life, you'll see that some do move their heads, some move the harmonica, and some do a combination of both. What's important is that you find a sound and technique that works for you.

Now let's add this slide to the front of the blues riff.

◆5 Slidin' Blues

Now let's add the extra note that you learned back in "Triplet Blues" to create your first authentic blues riff, as shown in "Lazy Blues."

◆6 Lazy Blues

Do you remember the "train whistle" technique from Lesson 6, **Book 1**? We're going to use the same technique to add a finishing touch to this blues riff.

❼ Blues on the Rail

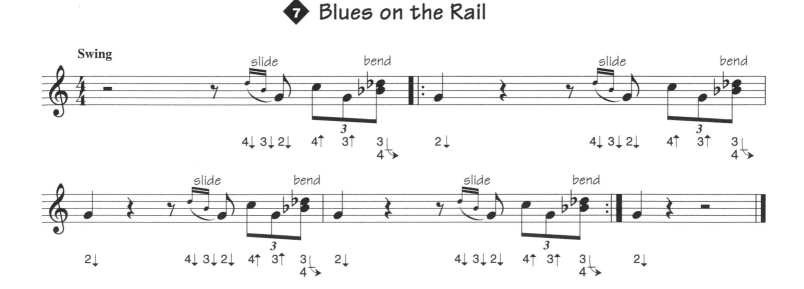

If you've mastered the slide, bend, and train whistle, then you're really playing the blues!

Posture

Right back at the beginning of **Book 1** you learned how to hold your harmonica. We've covered a lot of ground since then and sometimes bad habits can creep in, so let's review your playing position:

This is the traditional **C position**, so called because the left hand forms a "C" shape. To get an authentic blues sound, you're looking to create an airtight resonant chamber with your hands, which gives you great control over the sound quality.

Using a mirror, look at the back of your hands and check for any air leaks. You'll be able to hear when you've got a good seal—the sound will be slightly muffled, and when you open your hands, the sound will become brighter.

Once you've got your hand position sorted out, spend some time thinking about your overall body posture. Just like a singer, you must use your breath to power your instrument. Therefore, it's really important to adapt a good posture, as this will give you maximum control over your playing.

Stand up tall, with your shoulders back and head up. There is often a tendency to let the head droop forward, which should be resisted. Apart from anything else, you'll start to drool into your harmonica!

You may want to do some simple breathing exercises as part of your practice routine. These are a great warm-up, and will prepare you for a good harmonica workout.

An alternative hand position

If you study other harmonica players, you'll notice that some of them hook their thumbs over the edges of the harmonica on the left- and right-hand sides. Depending on the shape and size of your hands, you might find this a more comfortable playing position, and it might be easier to form an airtight chamber.

When done properly, the two hands leave a 'V' shape, which, when the harmonica is played, is filled by the chin, creating a bigger resonant chamber than is possible with the traditional "C" hand position.

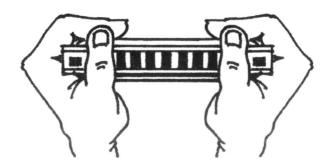

Experiment with both positions and see which feels most comfortable to you. Both have advantages and disadvantages, so it's really a matter of personal taste.

Maintenance: looking after your harp

It's good practice to clean your harp thoroughly on a regular basis; it's hygienic, and can help to prolong the life of the instrument. The chances are that you have a plastic-bodied harmonica (most beginners' instruments are plastic-bodied), and if so, the simplest and most effective way to clean your instrument is to run it under water, using a toothbrush to clean the mouthpiece thoroughly. (Don't do this with a wooden-bodied instrument as it will cause the wood to expand and may ruin it.)

Other hints and tips:

 Before playing, have a drink of water. This will remove any residues from sticky food or drinks that may make their way into the harmonica.

 After playing, knock the harmonica against your leg or the palm of your hand to remove any excess moisture.

 When not in use, keep your harmonica in its case. This will protect it from dust and dirt, as well as from accidental knocks and dents.

 Keep the instrument away from excessive heat or humidity.

For hygiene reasons, don't lend your harmonica to other players; equally, don't play other peoples' instruments.

Time to relax   take a break and go for a short walk.
When you return, review this chapter briefly before moving on.

LESSON 2
Draw bends and tongue blocking

Half-step draw bends

Back in **Book 1** we saw that there were draw bends available on holes 1–4 of the C harmonica:

Hole	1	2	3	4
Draw	D	G	B	D
Bend	Db/C#	Gb/F#	Bb/A#	Db/C#

These are all known as **half-step bends**, because the bent note in each case is a half step lower than the basic drawn note.

There's one more *half-step draw bend* that is available to us, which can be found on hole 6:

Hole	1	2	3	4	5	6
Draw	D	G	B	D	F	A
Bend	Db/C#	Gb/F#	Bb/A#	Db/C#		Ab/G#

Practice drawing on the 6th hole, and then bending down from A to Ab.

◆ 8 Half-step Shuffle

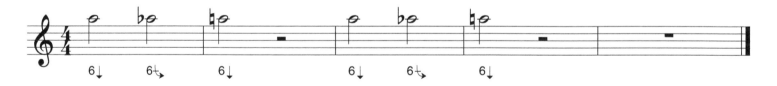

Once you've mastered this, try hitting the bent note first, and then move to the unbent note.

◆ 9 Shufflin' Down

Finally, practice the following exercise, which uses both A♭ and A. Try to hit the bent A♭ cleanly each time.

🔟 Take It Down

Invent similar exercises for the *half-step draw bends* on holes 1–4.

Whole-step draw bends

In Lesson 1, we saw that there are actually three draw bends available from the 3rd hole:

Hole	3
Draw	B
1st bend	B♭/A♯
2nd bend	A
3rd bend	A♭/G♯

The first bend is the half-step bend that you already know about, from B to B♭. The next bend is known as a **whole-step bend**; it goes from B to A. To get this bend, use the same technique as you did for the half-step bend, but do more of it! As mentioned in Lesson 1, try using the mouth shape "tee" for the half-step bend, and "too" for the whole-step bend. Give it a whirl in this next exercise.

1️⃣1️⃣ Breakin' the Blues

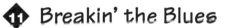

☞ HINT: For about the same price as a harmonica, it's now possible to buy a digital chromatic tuner, which is invaluable when practicing your bends. The tuner has a built-in microphone that detects the pitch of the note produced and converts it into a visual display. When practicing, use the tuner to make sure that you are hitting each bend cleanly and accurately.

Now try moving from the unbent note straight to the whole-step bend.

1️⃣2️⃣ Steppin' Down

Next, try hitting the whole-step bend first, before moving to the unbent note.

🔷13 Steppin' Up

Finally, combine both the half-step and whole-step bends in this next example.

🔷14 Only a Step Away

There's also a whole-step draw bend available on hole 2 (G), the note F.

Hole	2
Draw	G
1st bend	G♭/F♯
2nd bend	F

☞ HINT: It's easy to remember the pattern of bends on the first three holes.

    1st hole: 1 bend available

    2nd hole: 2 bends available

    3rd hole: 3 bends available

After that, it gets a bit more complicated!

Here are a couple of simple examples using both the half-step and whole-step bends on hole 2. **Track 15** shows how the notes might be used on a traditional blues track, and **Track 16** adds a little funk to the music!

🔷15 🔷16 Around the Corner

traditional funk
blues

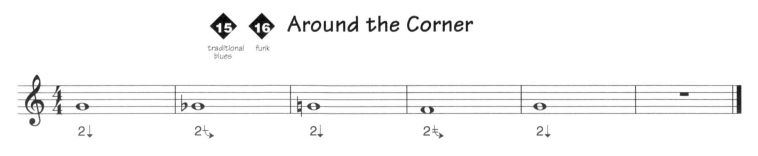

And finally, here's a piece that uses the bends on all of the first three holes.

🎵17 Why Don't We Go

Don't be tempted to move on to any of the later lessons until you've really mastered these bends. This may take some time, but don't get too despondent—keep practicing and you will get there!

Tongue blocking

In Lesson 1 of **Book 1** we introduced the **pucker method** to enable us to play single notes on the harmonica. This is a useful technique, but it's not the only way of achieving this effect. Many harmonica players employ an alternative method called **tongue blocking**. Put simply, this means using your tongue to block off certain holes (the clue is in the name!) to allow you to play single notes.

This has two distinct advantages:

 You can mix chords and single notes easily.

2 It allows a wider mouth shape, which improves tone.

In fact, some harmonica techniques and sounds are impossible to play without using tongue blocking.

You may think that using the tongue in this way will prevent you from bending notes, but this is not the case! In time, you will develop different techniques for bending, which will allow you both to bend notes and to use the tongue blocking method.

Let's start by using tongue blocking to isolate hole 4. Experiment with your tongue until you can cover holes 1–3 completely. You will find that in order to do this, the harmonica has to be placed much further into the mouth than for the pucker method. You might find that it helps to use the side of the tongue, with the harmonica tilted towards the right-hand side of the mouth.

The idea is that the hole you want to play is played from the right-hand side of the mouth, with the holes to the left blocked by the tongue.

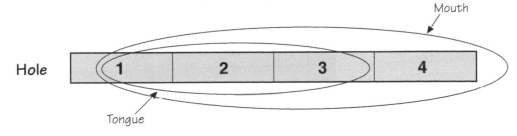

Let's try a simple example using tongue blocking. Get into the position as previously described, with your tongue blocking holes 1–3, leaving hole 4 open. Once you've isolated hole 4, try this tune, which uses only the draw and blow notes from hole 4.

⑱ A Whole Lotta Blues

The good news is that once you've perfected this position, it can be moved anywhere on the harmonica to produce single notes. Let's try this in the next tune, "Brother Jacques Rock."

⑲ Brother Jacques Rock

Now try "Home on the Range" from **Book 1**, which focuses on Zone 2 of the harmonica.

⑳ Home on the Range

Some players use only the pucker method, and some use only tongue blocking, while others use both. It's worth persevering with tongue blocking because it will allow you to get some effects that can't be produced in any other way.

LESSON 3
Blow bends

High-register bends

In Lesson 5 of **Book 1**, we explored using blow bends on the top three holes of the harmonica to access the notes E♭, G♭, and B♭ (holes 8, 9, and 10). However, just as there are multiple bends available on draws at the bottom end of the harmonica, there is one multiple bend available at the top end of the instrument, which allows you to reach the note B♭.

2nd bend			B♭
1st bend	E♭/D#	G♭/F#	C♭/B
Blow	E	G	C
Hole	8	9	10

Follow the instructions given on page 36 of **Book 1** and see if you can get the half-step *blow* bends on holes 8, 9, and 10. It's actually very difficult to get the half-step bend on hole 10 (C to B), and you may well find it easier to get this new whole-step bend (C to B♭).

21 Screamin' Blues

As before, you should also practice hitting the bent note first, before moving to the unbent note.

22 Way Up

23 Blue Bird Blues

15

The most famous exponent of the blow bend in blues harp playing is Jimmy Reed. A good starting point is the album *Big Boss Man: The Best of Jimmy Reed*.

☞ TIP: If you have a harmonica in a different key (say in G, or A), you may find it easier to obtain the blow bends. This is because the reeds at the top end of a C diatonic harmonica are very small, and it therefore requires very minute control of the mouth shape to force the bend.

The full story

Congratulations! You now know all the blow and draw bends on the diatonic harmonica. Here's a complete diagram showing all the bends:

2nd bend										B♭
1st bend								E♭	G♭	B
Blow	C	E	G	C	E	G	C	E	G	C
Hole	1	2	3	4	5	6	7	8	9	10
Draw	D	G	B	D	F	A	B	D	F	A
1st bend	D♭	G♭	B♭	D♭		A♭				
2nd bend		F	A							
3rd bend			A♭							

Now that you know where all the notes are, it's time for a couple of exercises to help you find them quickly.

Let's start by finding all the Cs on your harmonica.

◆24 Four Cs

Now try the Ds.

◆25 Three Ds

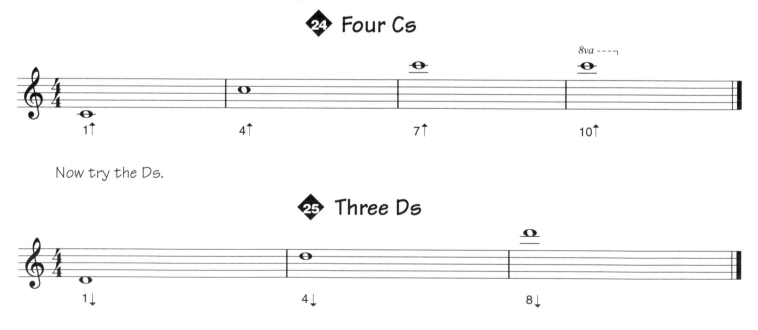

Repeat this exercise for all the other notes shown on the diagram, and then try the next exercise for a challenge!

◆26 All Notes

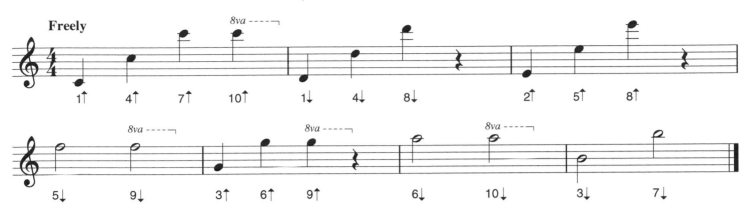

Once you've mastered this, try this ultimate octave challenge which requires use of accurate bending to extend the number of notes available.

◆27 All-note Challenge

Tongue blocking revisited

In the last lesson we introduced the technique of *tongue blocking*, with the note being played out of the right side of the mouth while the tongue blocks notes to the left. It is also possible to do the reverse; that is, to play notes out of the left side of the mouth, while blocking notes to the right.

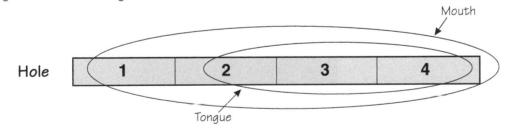

Get into the position described above, with your tongue blocking holes 2–4, leaving hole 1 open. Once you've isolated hole 1, try "Around the Block," which uses only the draw and blow notes from hole 1.

◆28 Around the Block

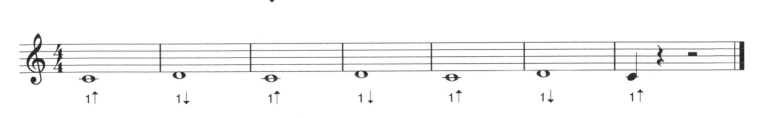

17

Just as before, this position can be moved anywhere on the harmonica to produce single notes. To prove it, try playing "Brother Jacques Rock" again, this time using the left-sided tongue blocking technique such that all notes are played with the left side of the mouth.

29 Brother Jacques Rock

4↑ 4↓ 5↑ 4↑ 4↑ 4↓ 5↑ 4↑ 5↑ 5↓ 6↑ 5↑ 5↓ 6↑

6↑ 5↓ 5↑ 4↑ 6↑ 5↓ 5↑ 4↑ 4↑ 4↓ 4↑ 4↑ 4↓ 4↑

Most players tend to use only the right-sided technique described in the previous lesson, but having both techniques in your musical armory will provide for maximum flexibility.

The ultimate use of the tongue blocking technique is to play out of both sides of the mouth at once, to play a two-note chord.

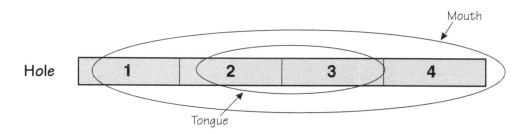

Follow the diagram above, placing your mouth over holes 1–4, with your tongue blocking holes 2–3. This allows you to blow or draw through holes 1 and 4 simultaneously, producing either octave Cs or Ds.

30 Double Up

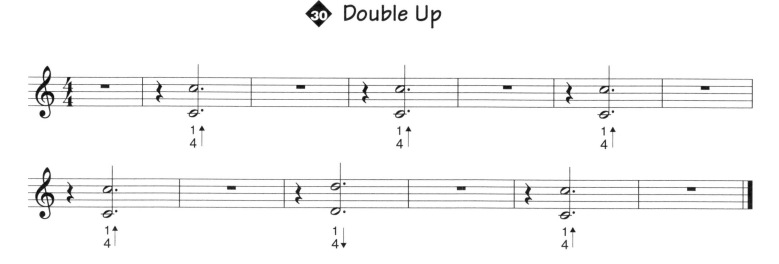

1↑
4↑

1↑
4↑

1↑
4↑

1↑
4↑

1↓
4↓

1↑
4↑

Of course, you don't have to block only the middle two holes; you can block one hole, or three holes, depending on the effect you want to create.

Next is a complete example that brings together all the tongue blocking techniques that we've introduced so far: playing out of the left and right sides of the mouth and using intervals. Look out for the bends in measures 1 and 3, played out of the right side and left side of the mouth, respectively.

31 ◆ All in One

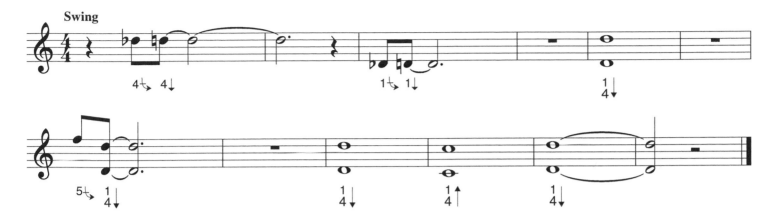

To finish, here's a great little tongue-blocking turnaround. Look out for the alternation between octaves and full chords, produced by blocking holes 2 and 3 with your tongue to produce the octave, and then removing the tongue to give the full chord.

32 ◆ Full-blown

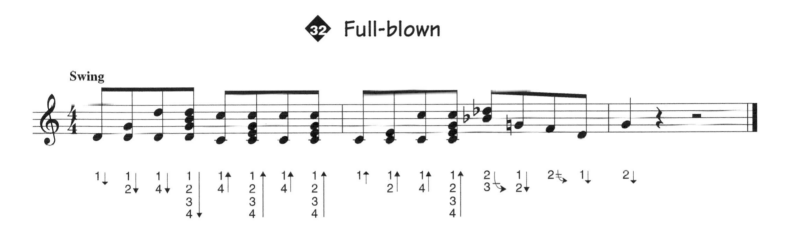

Was that tiring? Take a break and do a few stretching exercises.
You'll then be ready to hit Lesson 4, refreshed and relaxed.

LESSON 4
Using harps in different keys

Up to this point, all the exercises in this book and **Book 1** have been designed for the diatonic harmonica in C. You've now learned all the draw and blow notes on this harp, as well as all the draw and blow bends. You may be wondering what else there is left to learn!

Well, don't worry, because this is only the start. Diatonic harmonicas are available in every single key—all twelve of them. The reason for this is simply to make life easier for the harmonica player. As you saw back in **Book 1**, the diatonic harmonica is specifically designed to make it easy to play in the key of the harmonica. A lot of the hard work of note selection has already been done for you by the designer of the harmonica!

Typically, the range of harmonicas starts with G harp at the lowest end, and rises up to F harp at the top. Most music stores will stock these harps, but some specialist suppliers will also have "High G," "Low F," or even "Low D" harps.

Popular keys

Most players start with a C harmonica, because C major is the simplest key to learn. However, in practice, the most common harmonicas are probably the A and D diatonic harps, because these harmonicas enable you to play in keys favored by guitarists. In this chapter we'll assume that you have invested in both A and D harmonicas. If you only have a C harp, you'll still be able to learn the exercises, but you won't be able to play along with the audio, as all the backing tracks will be in the wrong key!

The A harmonica

Let's start with the blues riff that you learned back in Lesson 1, but played on the A harp instead of the C harp.

33 Slide Away Blues

THEORY TIP: Notice the four sharp (#) signs that appear at the beginning of this piece. This is a characteristic of pieces in E, and is called a **key signature**. It tells you that these notes (F, C, G, and D) should be sharp. However, even though the tune is in E, because this is a blues-based riff, we use an A harp. Often, when a blues tune is in a certain key, the key of the harp chosen is three steps up from that key. Thus a blues tune in G could use a harp in C. This is not always the case however: you could still use an A harp for a tune in the key of A. Don't worry too much about this yet. As long as you follow the harmonica notation below the staff, all the notes will be in the right key.

Make life easier for yourself

The key of the harmonica is not only important because it enables you to play in different keys. Different harmonicas also make different techniques easier or harder. For example, *blow bends* are generally easier on lower key instruments, so the G harp is usually considered the easiest for playing these. This is simply because the reeds on the G harp are longer than those on higher-key instruments. Conversely, the *draw bends* at the bottom of the G harp are more difficult than those on, say, a C harp.

Here's a simple blow-bend riff for a harmonica in A. In this case, the tune is actually in the key of A (the three-sharp key signature tells you this).

34 Riff Away

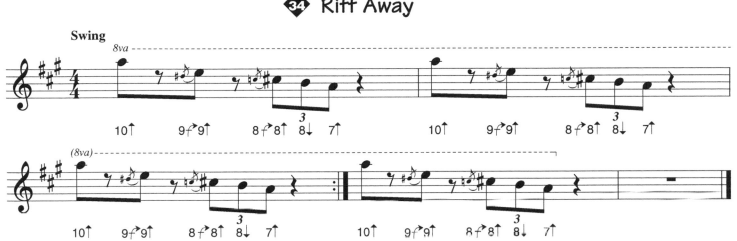

Notice the small notes preceding some of the larger ones. These are called **grace notes**, and indicate a quick note to ornament the main note. In this case, these grace notes are played first (as bends), and then the following main notes are kind of slid up to, or "unbent." Listening to the audio track will give you an idea how this sounds.

Try playing "Riff Away" on your C harmonica and see if it's easier or harder. Simply follow the same notation regarding holes, blow, draw, and bends.

☞ TIP: As you build up a range of instruments, practice bending on all of them to get used to the different feel required for each one.

Here's the complete note layout for the A harmonica:

2nd bend										G
1st bend								C	D♯	G♯
Blow	A	C♯	E	A	C♯	E	A	C♯	E	A
Hole	1	2	3	4	5	6	7	8	9	10
Draw	B	E	G♯	B	D	F♯	G♯	B	D	F♯
1st bend	A♯	D♯	G	A♯		F				
2nd bend		D	F♯							
3rd bend			F							

E is for easy

Now, for more about harp keys vs. the key of the song: Although guitarists do often like to play in A and D, generally their favorite key is E major, because the lowest string of the guitar is usually tuned to E. As we saw with "Slide Away Blues," you can use your A harmonica and play in **second position**, also known as **cross harp**.

You used the same technique back in Lesson 5 of **Book 1** to play in the key of G using a C harmonica. The root note of the key, in this case E, is found on draw 2, and this becomes your *home position* (also called **tonic**).

Try this chilled-out bluesy example in E major.

◆35◆ Chill Out

The D harmonica

Now let's look at your D harmonica. Here's the complete note layout.

2nd bend										C
1st bend								F	G♯	C♯
Blow	D	F♯	A	D	F♯	A	D	F♯	A	D
Hole	**1**	**2**	**3**	**4**	**5**	**6**	**7**	**8**	**9**	**10**
Draw	E	A	C♯	E	G	B	C♯	E	G	B
1st bend	D♯	G♯	C	D♯		B♭				
2nd bend		G	B							
3rd bend			A♯							

Now let's try a well-known folk tune in D, "Soldier's Joy." There are a lot of notes to get to grips with in this melody, so start slowly and build up speed until you can play along with the backing track.

36 Soldier's Joy

THEORY TIP: This example has a key signature of two sharps, which is used for tunes in D major. If you want to work out the key of a piece with a sharp key signature, just go up a half step from the last sharp sign. In this case, the last sharp is C#, so the key is D major. Check the pieces you've just played in A and E to make sure that this works.

And now let's try using the D harp in second position to play in the key of A.

37 A Blue Swing

D harp

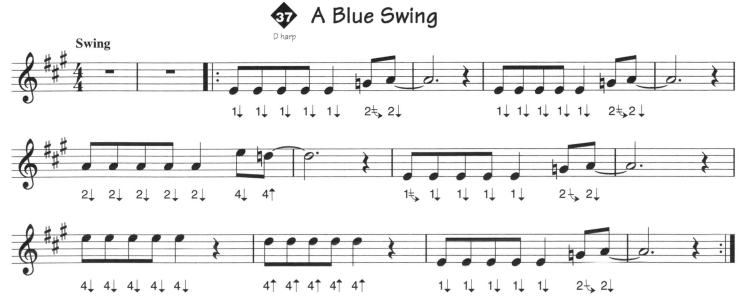

Of course, you could also play this tune in first position on the A harp. (This is basically the same tune, with a few small changes.)

🔶38 A New Blue Swing

A harp

When you get to the end of this book, you'll find three great tunes with which you can play along. They integrate with all the other books in the **FastTrack®** series, so you can get together and jam with other musicians using the same books. These three songs require diatonic harmonicas in the keys of E♭, A, and D.

Playing with other instruments

You've already used harmonicas in D and A, which are great for playing with guitarists. An E♭ harmonica is useful if you're going to be playing with brass or wind players, whose instruments are often in either B♭ (trumpet, tenor sax, clarinet) or E♭ (alto sax).

Articulation

Back in **Book 1** we introduced the concept of tonguing. This is not to be confused with tongue blocking, which we talked about back in Lesson 3. From now on, to avoid confusion, we will use the term *articulation* to describe tonguing techniques.

Articulation is all about how you can control the beginning of each note that you play. This is the most important part of the note, and gives it a huge part of its sound. Articulation is an important part of playing any wind instrument, whether it's a flute, oboe, or harmonica.

In **Book 1** you used the sound "ta" to give a strong attack to the beginning of the note. Say the consonant "t" and notice where the tongue is in your mouth as you say it—you should find that it's very close to the front of the mouth. Now try saying "k," and you'll find that the tongue has moved further back in the mouth.

Experiment with using these two consonants to shape the attacks of notes on the harmonica. Here's an example that uses simple repeated chords: try saying "ta-ka-ta-ka" to articulate each note separately. (We're now back on the C harmonica.)

24

◈39 Ta-ka I

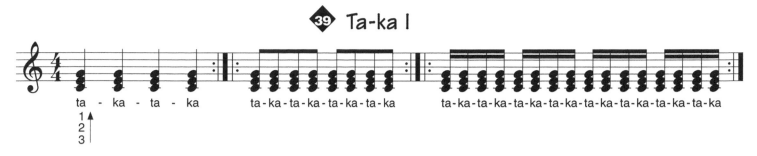

ta - ka - ta - ka   ta-ka-ta-ka-ta-ka   ta-ka-ta-ka-ta-ka-ta-ka-ta-ka-ta-ka-ta-ka-ta-ka

You can use this articulation pattern for both blow and draw notes. To start with, it will feel more natural to do it when playing blow notes, after all, we all use consonants when we speak. However, it works just as well with draw notes. Work on this next example until you can play it just as well as the previous one.

◆40 Ta-ka II

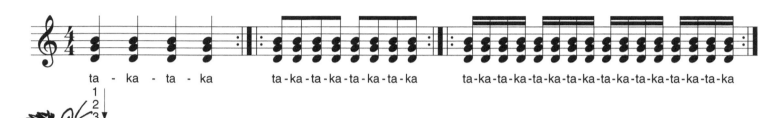

ta - ka - ta - ka   ta-ka-ta-ka-ta-ka-ta-ka   ta-ka-ta-ka-ta-ka-ta-ka-ta-ka-ta-ka-ta-ka

LISTENING TIP: Rhythmic playing of this type was a key component of Sonny Terry's distinctive style. Check out the title track on his album *Whoopin' the Blues* to hear it in action.

These two consonants work well because it's easy to switch from "t" to "k" and back again. When you need to play triplets (which, as we've seen, are commonly found in blues tunes), you can use other combinations of consonants. Try the following example and experiment with different groupings, such as "ta-da-ka" or "ta-da-la."

◆41 Ta-da-ka

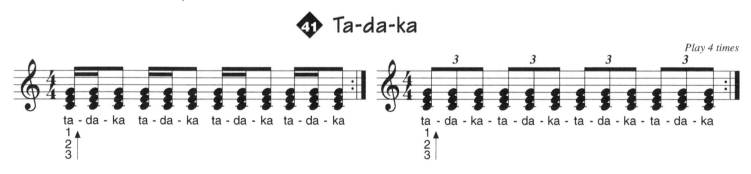

Play 4 times

ta - da - ka   ta - da - ka   ta - da - ka   ta - da - ka   ta - da - ka - ta - da - ka - ta - da - ka - ta - da - ka

And again, try the same thing with draw notes. This time, start with slow triplets before trying some faster ones.

◆42 Slow Then Fast

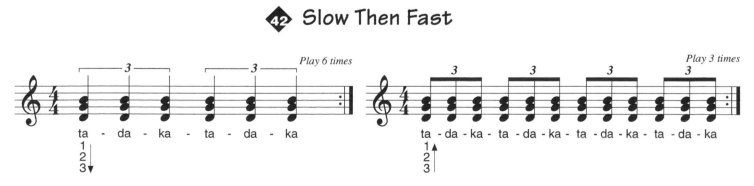

Play 6 times   *Play 3 times*

ta - da - ka - ta - da - ka   ta - da - ka - ta - da - ka - ta - da - ka - ta - da - ka

Now try combining some of these rhythms with various consonants. Some possibilities are included in the next example, below the score, but experiment and find out which ones work best for you. The key consonants are those that involve the tongue but not the lips, so concentrate on "t," "d," "k," and even "g."

43 Rhythm Challenge

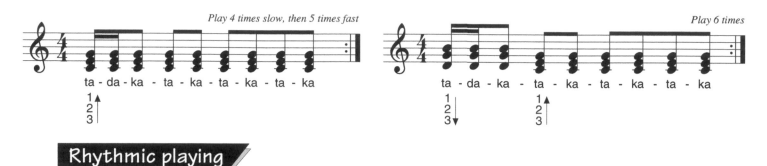

Rhythmic playing

In the early days of the harmonica, it was used primarily as a chordal instrument to accompany singing or other instrumental lines. However, as time passed, people tended to explore its melodic possibilities, such that it has become more of a lead instrument. But some styles of harmonica music do indeed feature rhythmic playing prominently, particularly the old-time music from the 1920s and '30s. For examples of this style check out the album *Harmonica Masters* (YAZCD2019).

As we've seen, articulation is a key technique to master when playing rhythmic parts. Next, we're going to learn a great rhythmic backing style that's versatile enough to use for accompanied or unaccompanied playing.

44 Back Again

Start by playing this simple shuffle rhythm, drawing on holes 1, 2, and 3. Next add some articulation, using the mouth shapes "ta-do" as you play the rhythm; pucker your lips forward on the second note of each pair so that you are only drawing on hole 2.

Now, let's speed it up a bit and vary the pattern.

45 Return to Blue

Practice this and try to keep the rhythm steady and even; remember that the purpose of rhythms like this in unaccompanied playing is to set the tempo and beat. Once you've got this main rhythmic pattern absolutely steady, you can interrupt it with short blues phrases or *licks*, like this:

46 Been Gone

Once you've played the lick, don't forget to return to the rhythmic pattern to keep the beat going.

A different approach to this style of rhythmic backing would be to use tongue blocking to alternate between chords and single notes.

In the next example, single notes alternate with *draw chords* to give the illusion of a melody with accompaniment. Start by playing the "ta-do" rhythm, but use tongue blocking to isolate the second note in each pair.

47 Long Gone

Now try moving this pattern up to holes 3–4.

48 Miss Me?

We can then extend the pattern further into a familiar boogie sequence.

49 I'll Be Back

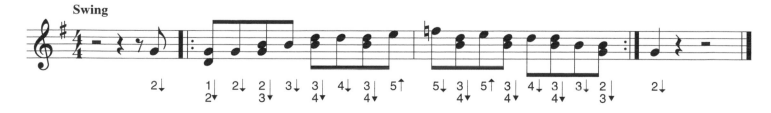

Dynamics

Dynamics is a word that musicians use to describe how loud or quiet to play. A tune that has both very quiet and very loud sections is said to have a wide dynamic range. For example, the verse of a song might be quiet, before the chorus slams in and the volume level jumps up.

A lot of bands out there only play at one dynamic level: VERY VERY LOUD. Don't get me wrong, there's nothing wrong with loud music, but if you're after the maximum emotional impact from your music, then you should really experiment with different dynamic levels, both within a single song, and also across different songs in your set list.

For example, you might want to program your set list so that you start with a couple of loud, up-tempo numbers, before bringing the dynamic level down a bit for a sensitive ballad. Apart from giving you a chance to recharge your energy levels, this strategy also means that when you slam into your fourth song at full volume, it's going to have a huge impact.

Dynamic Symbols

Musicians use a set of simple symbols to represent different dynamic levels, based on Italian terms. In Italian, *piano* means "quiet," so we use the symbol *p* to mean quiet. *Forte* means "loud," so we use the symbol *f*. And if we want to get louder or quieter, we just add more *f*s or *p*s, so:

> *ff* = very loud
> *fff* = very, very loud
> *ffff* = My ears are bleeding, go away!
>
> *pp* = very quiet
> *ppp* = very, very quiet
> *pppp* = What?

Using varied dynamics can turn a one-dimensional performance into something much more interesting. The simplest way to achieve dynamic effects with the harmonica is to vary the position of your hand. By doing this you are affecting the size of the resonant cavity and the quality of the airtight seal achieved. Experiment to see how softly you can play a note, and then try gradually to increase the volume through a combination of blowing or drawing more forcefully and altering the size of the resonant cavity.

 TIP: Put less wind through your instrument when playing high notes, as it is possible to damage these smaller reeds.

LESSON 5
Playin' the blues

Back in **Book 1** you learned about two different types of scales: the major and the minor. In pop, rock, jazz, and blues, many other different types of scales are used.

The blues scale

In blues, there's only one scale that you need to know, and (surprise!) it's called the blues scale. The blues scale in C is shown in the following example. Listen to **Track 50** to hear what this sounds like.

50 C Blues Scale

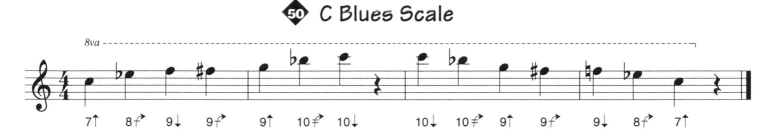

Note that this scale is only available in the top octave in first position.

While it is possible to play blues harmonica in *first*, *second*, and even *third positions*, it's most commonly played in *second position*. The reason for this is that there are more bends available, giving the player the maximum number of choices when playing the blues.

Here's the blues scale in *second position* (i.e., in G on a C harmonica). Practice this slowly until you can hit all the bends directly.

51 G Blues Scale

If you're having trouble with these bends, you might like to try playing the blues scale in *third position* (i.e., in D on a C harmonica).

52 D Blues Scale

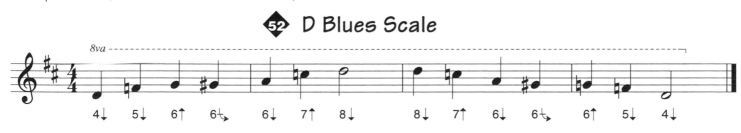

Once you're happy with the basic blues scale, try a simple blues melody, as in "Simple Life."

53 Simple Life

The notes in the blues scale that sound the most bluesy are called the **blue notes** (the second, fourth, and sixth notes in the blues scale). By emphasizing these notes, you can get the maximum blues power out of your harmonica, and the best way to do this is by playing those notes as bends.

Playing the G blues scale in *second position*, the two blue notes that can be played as bends are the B♭ and D♭ (or C♯). **Track 54** is just like **Track 51**, but played slower so you can really hear the bluesy quality to the bent notes.

54 G Blues Scale (slow)

The other key blue note in this blues scale is F, which can be found as a *whole step bend* on draw 2. Look out for the *blue notes* (C♯, B♭, and F) in the next example and emphasize them as you play to create the maximum blues power!

55 On My Way

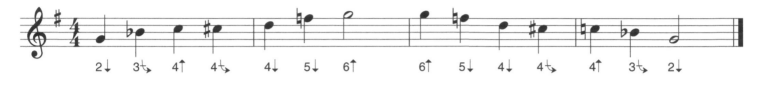

Note that this tune is nearly the same as "Simple Life," but with a C♯ instead of a D in the opening measure to bring another blue note into the melody.

Jammin': the 12-bar blues sequence

The 12-bar blues is a classic chord sequence that's been used by blues musicians since the year dot. Once you know your way around a 12-bar, you'll be able to sit in on a blues session anywhere in the world—it's a universal form that all blues musicians know.

A typical 12-bar sequence in G might look like this:

Bar	1	2	3	4	5	6	7	8	9	10	11	12
Chord	G7	C7	G7	G7	C7	C7	G7	G7	D7	C7	G7	G7

Try it out yourself with "Clockin' In."

56 Clockin' In

Until "Clockin' In," the blues examples you've played so far have used only two chords, known as **I** and **IV** because they're constructed from the first and fourth notes of the major scale. In "Clockin' In," G7 is the I chord and C7 is the IV. This makes life easy because the blues scale works over both these chords; as long as you choose notes from the blues scale, whatever you play will sound good.

However, we've now got a new chord in our sequence, D7, or **V**. Unfortunately, the standard G blues scale won't sound great over this chord. But don't panic! On page 29, you learned the blues scale in D, which you played in *third position*. So all you need to do is switch from the G blues scale to the D blues scale when you get to the D chord in the sequence.

Learn the layout of the 12-bar blues sequence until you know exactly where the V chord occurs—it has a distinctive sound in the context of the sequence.

Next, we have a complete blues backing track in G. Experiment for yourself using the blues scales given on p. 29. Make up your own riffs and hear how they fit over the I, IV, and V chords.

57 Blues Backing Track

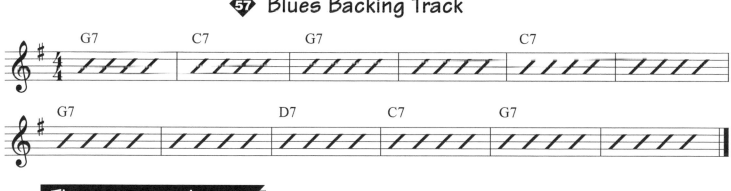

The turnaround

The **turnaround** is the name for the short section at the end of the blues sequence that prepares us for the start of a new 12-bar section. It "turns around" the sequence, hence the name. Typically the turnaround involves moving from the I chord to the IV chord, and then the V chord, before returning to I again for the start of a new 12-bar sequence. There are many standard turnaround phrases and licks that you can learn in advance, which can then just be dropped into a blues jam as you need them.

Here is a classic example:

58 Turnaround

Here's a complete 12-bar sequence with a turnaround. Experiment yourself and see what you can come up with!

◆59 12-Bar Blues with Turnaround

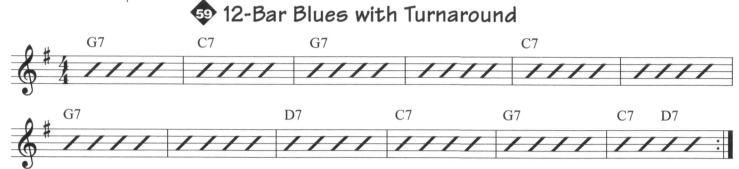

What if I don't know what to play?

Improvisation often sounds scary to beginners.

Here are a few tips to help you as you start to jam:

1. If all else fails, play the root note of the chord: over a G chord play G.

2. If you're stuck, then tremolo. If you're playing in *second position* and you're stuck for something to play over the V chord, then alternating rapidly between draws on 4 and 5 produces a really authentic blues sound.

3. You don't have to play all the time. If you don't have anything to play, then don't be afraid to shut up!

4. Use *call* and *response*: Pick up on phrases or licks that other members of the band are playing and imitate them.

5. Repetition is good! Many musicians assume that it's bad to repeat phrases over and over again, but nothing could be further from the truth.

More hand effects!

The hand wah

Back in Lesson 6 of **Book 1**, we introduced the hand vibrato, which is a great technique for adding interest to your playing. Also, the technique of using your hand to shape the sound of each note by opening and closing the resonating cavity to give a "wah" sound is very flexible and can be used to add expression to individual notes.

It's really important to form an airtight seal with your hands—that's the only way that you'll get this distinctive sound. Do a visual check on your hands for any gaps, all the way around, and listen for air escaping.

Listen to **Track 60** and then have a go yourself, blowing on the third hole.

◆60

If you got it, try "Wah Do You Know?"

◆61 Wah Do You Know?

Fanning

This technique is basically a *wah* speeded up. It is similar to *vibrato*, a technique used by most singers and instrumentalists. This example also includes a bend.

62 Fanning

Finally, let's put everything together: the *wah*, a *bend*, and the *fanning* technique.

63 Together Again

The hand wah is an incredibly expressive technique, and by varying the speed and timing of the wah, you can get some fantastic effects. In many ways it can be even more effective than a singer's vibrato, in that you can change the speed, depth, and intensity, all on one note!

 LISTENING TIP: The hand *wah* was a favorite technique of Sonny Boy Williamson II, and you can hear it on just about every track he recorded. Check out the track "Cool, Cool Blues" from the album *King Biscuit Time*.

The hand smack

Try playing a draw bend on 4, and as you release the bend, hit the harmonica on the right-hand side with your right hand, pushing the instrument to the left, so that you are now drawing on holes 4–5. If you keep your left hand firmly in position, the harmonica will spring back after you hit it, so that you'll once again be drawing only on hole 4.

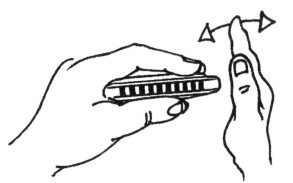

Track 64 demonstrates the hand smack—take a listen.

WARNING! When attempting this technique, please don't use excessive force. Start gently; otherwise, your teeth could suffer!

This technique is particularly associated with Sonny Terry. Listen to "Airplane Blues" from his album *Whoopin' the Blues* to hear it in full effect.

LESSON 6
Jamming: minor keys

Natural minor scale

Back in Lesson 7 of **Book 1**, you learned about another type of key, the minor key. Just like the blues scale, the minor scale has its own unique sound, usually characterized as sad. In fact, there are three different types of minor scale, but the most useful one for harp players is known as the natural minor. It looks like this:

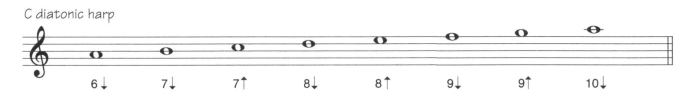

With your new knowledge of bends, it's now possible to play this scale over two octaves.

🔷65 Two-octave A Natural Minor Scale

Just like the blues scale, the *natural minor scale* can be used as the basis for improvisation. And just like the blues scale, some notes are more important than others, and give the scale its unique flavor. In the A natural minor scale, these notes are A, C, and G.

Try jamming over the following backing track using the A natural minor scale. If you find this daunting, then just focus on the important notes in the scale, as listed above. Once you're comfortable with them, try expanding your collection of notes to include the others.

🔷66

Let's try playing in another minor key, D minor. Here's the D natural minor scale:

🔷67 D Natural Minor Scale

Try to make the bends on the 3rd hole clean and distinct. Make sure to practice the scale both up and down. Once you're confident with the scale, try this famous melody that we played in **Book 1** (see page 42). Back then you played it in E minor, but this time we'll do it in D minor, using the scale above.

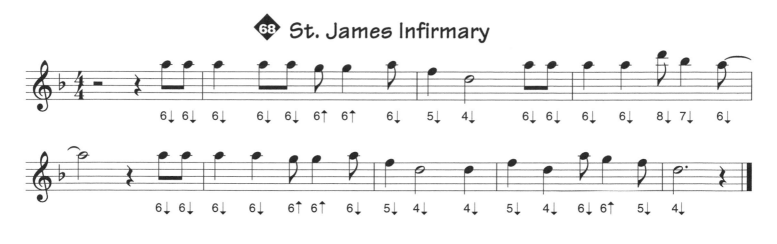

68 St. James Infirmary

6↓ 6↓ 6↓   6↓ 6↓ 6↑ 6↑   6↓ 5↓ 4↓   6↓ 6↓ 6↓ 6↓ 8↓ 7↓ 6↓

6↓ 6↓ 6↓ 6↓ 6↑ 6↑ 6↓ 5↓ 4↓   4↓ 5↓ 4↓ 6↓ 6↑ 5↓ 4↓

Natural-minor-tuned harmonicas

To make things easier, most harmonica manufacturers (Lee Oskar, Hohner) produce harps tuned to the natural minor scale. Here's a note layout for a harmonica tuned to A natural minor, which is designed to be played in *cross harp*.

Blow	D	F	A	D	F	A	D	F	A	D
Hole	1	2	3	4	5	6	7	8	9	10
Draw	E	A	C	E	G	B	C	E	G	B

The harp is designed in such a way that minor chords are easy to play. For example, the key chord of D minor is available on the blow notes, and A minor and E minor are available on the draw notes.

D minor chords:

Blow	D	F	A	D	F	A	D	F	A	D
Hole	1	2	3	4	5	6	7	8	9	10
Draw	E	A	C	E	G	B	C	E	G	B

A minor chord:

Blow	D	F	A	D	F	A	D	F	A	D
Hole	1	2	3	4	5	6	7	8	9	10
Draw	E	A	C	E	G	B	C	E	G	B

E minor chord:

Blow	D	F	A	D	F	A	D	F	A	D
Hole	1	2	3	4	5	6	7	8	9	10
Draw	E	A	C	E	G	B	C	E	G	B

Using a natural-minor harmonica will make jamming a lot easier, especially if you're not that confident with your bends. They're not used that often by blues players, but if you're into jazz or folk playing, then they're a worthwhile investment.

LESSON 7
Amplified harmonica

The harp is a great instrument to play acoustically, but it really comes into its own when electrified. We all recognize the classic sound of a wailing blues harmonica, and we've already covered many of the techniques required to play in this style. But if you really want to create that unique sound, you're going to need to invest in some gear as well.

Gear

In a band situation, you're going to need some amplification to be heard over the drums, bass, guitar, and any other instruments in your lineup. The classic setup usually features a **Fender Bassman** amp, together with an **Astatic JT30** microphone, although this has recently been discontinued. A good alternative mic would be the **Shure Green Bullet** (520DX).

Fender Bassman 100

Shure Green Bullet Microphone

This pro setup doesn't come cheap, and we wouldn't recommend spending a huge amount of money to start with. So if you're taking your first steps into the world of amplified blues harp, the following are a few things to look out for.

Amp

- Valve amplification
- Low wattage (because you want to overdrive the amp)
- Smaller speakers (it's better to have a cabinet with several small speakers than one large one, to reduce feedback)
- Reverb (if you like that sound); if your amp doesn't have a reverb, then dedicated reverb pedals are available (Electro Harmonix Holy Grail)

Examples of more affordable amps would be Fender Champ, Gibson Skylark, or the Kustom 12A.

Gibson Skylark

Kustom 12A

Mic

Mic choice is an intensely personal issue, but key factors to consider include:

- Style: Bullet ('50s-style hand-held, e.g., Green Bullet), stick (traditional vocal or instrument mic, i.e., SM57), or miniature condenser (i.e., Suzuki MS100) mics can be used.

Shure SM57

- Element type: Dynamic (cleaner), crystal (crunchier), or condenser.
- Comfort: You're going to be holding this mic for several hours in a gig situation, so make sure it's comfortable. Not only that, you need to make sure that you can create an air-tight seal around the mic and harp (see below).

Ebay is often a good place to start if you're looking for a vintage mic bargain.

If possible, try different combinations of amp and mic before you buy. At the end of the day, it's a very personal choice: you should buy the gear that gives you the sound you want.

Amplified harp technique

Holding the mic

The bullet-style mic is the most common choice for amplified harp. Start with the mic cupped between your two hands, facing towards you.

open cup

closed

Now put your harmonica in place, held between the thumb and forefinger of the left hand. As with the hand wah technique, you are looking to create an airtight seal around the mic and harmonica, so watch for any gaps and listen for the sound of air escaping.

Developing good tone

Remember, the sound that comes out of your amp is only as good as the sound that goes in! At this stage, you'll want to start seriously working on your tone, because the better you sound unamplified, the better you'll sound when you plug in.

Developing good tone will only come with playing, so take time to listen with a critical ear to the masters and try to emulate their sound, playing your harp every chance you get.

When playing amplified, you can let the amplifier do the work and play quite softly and still get a great sound. Players such as Little Walter often used this technique to great effect.

Getting the classic blues sound, but avoiding feedback

Ideally, you want your amp set so that it's over-driving (as much *gain* as you can), but not feeding back. If you keep getting feedback, try the following:

- Reduce the treble setting on the amp.
- Try not to have the amp directly behind you.
- Raise the amp off the floor (on a couple of beer crates, for example).
- Connect the amp to the PA via the "line out" jack.

LESSON 8
Overblows and overdraws

Missing notes and the chromatic scale

You've come a long way and learned a lot about the world of harmonica playing. You've mastered bends and have learned to get a lot of notes out of your diatonic harmonica. As we saw back in Lesson 3, by using *draw* and *blow bends*, it's possible to get many notes out of a diatonic harp in C. (See page 16 for diagram.)

However, you may have noticed that there are certain notes that don't appear anywhere on the diagram. In fact, there are twelve possible notes, which, when put in order, are called the **chromatic scale**. Almost all western classical music, as well as most rock, pop, folk, and jazz is created from these twelve notes. When they're written out they look like this:

If we compare this list of twelve notes to the diagram on page 16, we notice that the following notes are missing from the C diatonic harp: E♭ in the first octave; E♭, G♭, and B♭ in the second octave; and D♭ and A♭ in the top octave. It can be frustrating for harp players to realize that there are certain notes that their instrument can't play. Well, I have good news and bad news for you. The good news is that the harmonica *can* play these missing notes. The bad news is that it is difficult and requires you to set up your harmonica in a special way.

The overblow

A brief history

The technique we use for reaching these notes is called **overblowing**, a term coined by Howard Levy. An overblow doesn't require any more force than a normal bend, so the name is slightly misleading.

The physical explanation of the overblow is too complex to go into here. For the time being, all you need to know is that the overblow is a way of accessing notes that are otherwise not available on the diatonic harmonica.

Preparing your harp for overblows

Some harmonicas will *overblow* more easily than others—the dimensions of the reeds within the harmonica are crucial. The Hohner Golden Melody is favored as an *overblow* instrument.

Before attempting the overblow, you'll need to make sure your instrument is set up properly. This is a delicate process that needs to be undertaken with great care, as you can easily render your harmonica unplayable. It's worth starting with a cheap (or old) harp, so that you can perfect your technique before trying it on your favorite instrument!

What we are looking to achieve in order to allow *overblowing* is for the reed gap (i.e., the gap between the reed and the reed plate) to be small. Exactly how small the gap needs to be is a process of trial and error. If it's too small, the reed will choke and not play, but if it's too wide, the *overblow* will not be possible. You won't need to use this technique on holes 2, 3, or 7, so we can ignore these holes when adjusting the reed gaps.

1. Unscrew the cover plates from the harp and remove them.

2. First, adjust the draw reeds (the reeds on the bottom of the instrument). Very carefully, using a small screwdriver or toothpick, gently press down on the reed, pushing it towards the reed plate. After each adjustment, test to ensure that the hole still plays easily without choking up. If choking occurs, adjust the reed back again by inserting the screwdriver into the comb and pushing upwards.

3. Next, adjust the blow reeds in a similar fashion by inserting the screwdriver into the comb and pushing upwards. Again, test and adjust as necessary.

4. Replace the cover plates.

How to do it

WARNING: This technique isn't easy! It's going to take a lot of practice and perseverance to get all the overblows (and overdraws) that are available.

Start by gently blowing hole 6, then make a noise like white noise (radio static), or the crackle of a walkie-talkie, made with a hard "k" consonant sound at the beginning. This pushes up the back of the tongue and constricts the air flow. Listen to **Track 73** to hear the sort of sound we're talking about.

If you've adjusted the reeds properly, and have the right mouth shape, you should hear the note B♭ pop up from the normal blow note of G. With practice, and if you use the "k" articulation, you should be able to go straight to the B♭ without hearing the G at all.

As the chart on page 40 shows, you can use the same technique on holes 1, 4, and 5 to get the notes low B♭, G♭ and middle E♭. Start at hole 6 and work your way down the instrument. The overblows on the lower notes are more difficult. Listen to the following audio tracks to hear the sound of the overblows played correctly:

69 Overblow Hole 6   **72** Overblow Hole 1

70 Overblow Hole 5   **73** White-noise Technique

71 Overblow Hole 4

Overblow	E♭			E♭	G♭	B♭				
2nd bend										B♭
1st bend								E♭	G♭	B
Blow	C	E	G	C	E	G	C	E	G	C
Hole	1	2	3	4	5	6	7	8	9	10
Draw	D	G	B	D	F	A	B	D	F	A
1st bend	D♭	G♭	B♭	D♭		A♭				
2nd bend		F	A							
3rd bend			A♭							
Overdraw							D♭		A♭	D♭

Please note that, although we have not included any written musical examples for the *overblow* at this time, the tablature symbol used to indicate this will be a sideways, right-facing arrow. The *overdraw*, which we will discuss next, will be indicated by a sideways, left-facing arrow. These are also indicated in the tablature legend at the beginning of this book.

Overdraws

You may have noticed that the diagram above also lists *overdraws*. This is essentially the same technique as the overblow, except that you are drawing air *in* instead of blowing out. In this case, start at hole 7 and try making a noise like the one demonstrated on **Track 73**, which will constrict the back of the throat area. Again, if the harmonica has been set up properly and you have the correct mouth/throat shape, the overdraw note (D♭) will pop up from the normal draw note (B). With enough practice, it should be possible to hit the D♭ directly. Once you've mastered the overdraw on hole 7, work your way up to holes 9 and 10. Listen to the following tracks to hear the sound of the overdraws played correctly:

74 Overdraw Hole 7

75 Overdraw Hole 9

76 Overdraw Hole 10

Don't despair!

It may feel like you are never going to master this technique. If so, don't despair. Here are a couple of hints to make it easier:

- You can buy specially customized harmonicas that have been set up specifically for overblowing and overdrawing. Although these won't help you to perfect the technique, they will at least remove the possibility that your instrument is not set up properly, and once you have mastered the technique, they will give a better tone.

- Remember that many harp players go their whole lives without needing to use an overblow or overdraw. Of course, if you want to play chromatic jazz on a diatonic harp, you'll need this technique, but if you just want to play blues harp, you may never need it.

LESSON 9
The chromatic harmonica

Way back at the beginning of **Book 1**, we promised that we would cover the chromatic harmonica in Book 2, so here it is!

We've seen that it is possible, by using *overblows* and *overdraws* to play all 12 notes of the chromatic scale on the diatonic harmonica. However, as you've probably already discovered, it isn't easy, and the tone quality of some of the overblows isn't great. That's because the diatonic harp wasn't designed to play outside of its own key—hence the name diatonic.

Fortunately, the chromatic harmonica (as its name suggests) was designed specifically for this purpose. If you've ever heard the music of Larry Adler or Stevie Wonder, you'll be familiar with the sound of this wonderful instrument.

Typically, chromatic harps are substantially more expensive than diatonic instruments (three to four times the price), although cheap Far Eastern instruments are available.

Chromatic harmonic

How does it work?

The chromatic harmonica is basically two harmonicas sandwiched together, with a slide that directs air into either one. One harmonica is in the key of C and the other is in the key of C#, thus ensuring that all twelve notes of the chromatic scale are available in every octave.

Despite the fact that all twelve chromatic pitches are available, chromatic harmonicas do come in different keys. We recommend that you start with a twelve-hole chromatic harmonica in C. Sixteen-hole (four-octave) instruments are also available.

Note layout

In some ways, the note layout on the chromatic harp is simpler than it is on the diatonic harp, because the same pattern is repeated across all three octaves (with the exception of some instruments, where the upper range is extended to D, played as a draw on hole 12 with the side in).

Here's the complete note layout:

Blow, slide in	C#	F	G#	C#	C#	F	G#	C#	C#	F	G#	C#
Blow, slide out	C	E	G	C	C	E	G	C	C	E	G	C
Hole	1	2	3	4	5	6	7	8	9	10	11	12
Draw, slide out	D	F	A	B	D	F	A	B	D	F	A	B
Draw, slide in	D#	F#	A#	C	D#	F#	A#	C	D#	F#	A#	C

Holding the chromatic harp

The chromatic harmonica is substantially bigger than a diatonic instrument, and requires a slightly different hold to allow access to the *slide* button on the right-hand side.

The left-hand position is similar to the diatonic C hold, with the instrument wedged between the thumb and forefinger. The right hand makes a resonating chamber, with the forefinger extended to reach the slide button. Your two thumbs should end up pointing in roughly the same direction.

Playing the instrument

Before playing the instrument it's necessary to warm it up—hold it between your hands or stick it in your pocket for a couple of minutes before playing. This prevents condensation from building up inside the instrument, which can cause the valves to stick.

It's these valves that direct the air to the reeds; this means that, unlike the diatonic harmonica, all the breath through the hole is directed to one reed (either the draw or blow reed). For this reason, the chromatic harmonica must not be played with too much force, as this will cause damage.

Tongue blocking is the preferred playing technique for the chromatic harmonica. Refer back to pages 13–14 for an explanation of this technique. You may find that you have to modify your technique slightly to accommodate the larger holes of the chromatic instrument.

Getting started

We only have room for a very quick sampler on how to play chromatic harmonica, so if you want to know more, why not try *The Hal Leonard Complete Harmonica Method: Chromatic Harmonica* (HL00841286).

You learned to play the C major scale on the diatonic harp back on page 18 of **Book 1**. Here's some more good news: You can play exactly the same scale on the chromatic harp; the only difference is that you start at hole 5, not hole 4. The next examples don't require you to use the slide at all.

77 C Major Scale on Chromatic Harp

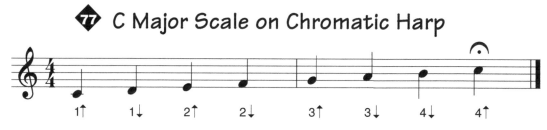

Even more good news: Unlike on the diatonic harp, this pattern can be repeated across all three octaves of the chromatic without any changes, starting at hole 1.

78 Three-octave C Major Scale

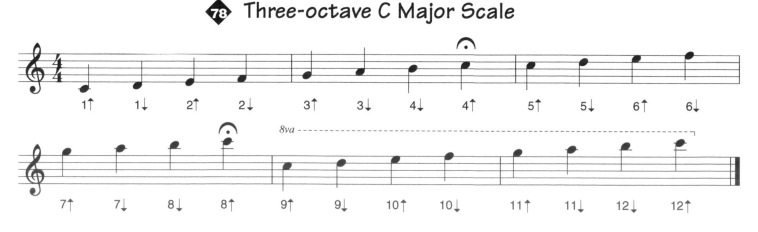

Back in **Book 1** you also learned to play a G major scale, but now we're going to show you a different way of playing it, on the chromatic harmonica.

The F#, which on the diatonic harp has to be played as a bend (in the top and bottom octaves), or overblow (in the middle octave), is easy to play on the chromatic harp. The F, which you would normally get by drawing on hole 6, is converted into an F# by pressing the slide button. When a note should be played with the button pushed in, like our F# here, it is indicated by a "+" sign next to the arrow.

79 G Major Scale on Chromatic Harp

Now try this melody in G, watching out for the F#s. Try to press the slide in neatly and quickly, and avoid catching the notes before or after the F#. You will need to press the slide button very slightly before you start to play the note.

80 Back Home

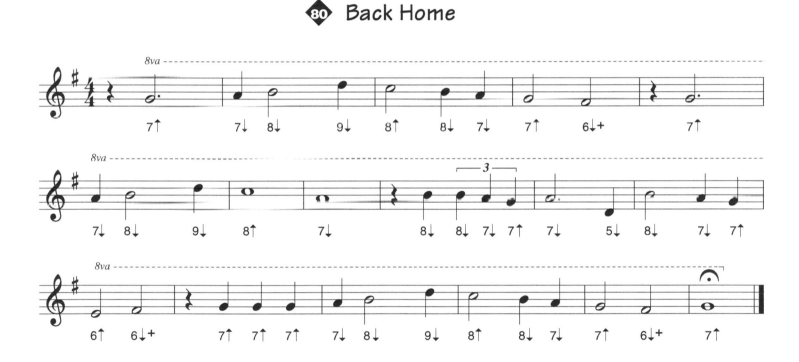

Now let's try another scale, D major. In this case you need to press the slide button for two notes, the F# and the C#.

81 D Major Scale

43

Finally, try this example in D major, looking out for all the C#s and F#s.

82 One-way Trip

WELL DONE!

We've covered a huge amount of material in this book, and the techniques and styles explained should keep you going for years! Remember that the main reason for playing the harmonica is to have fun and to develop your own style—don't worry too much if there are certain techniques that you don't seem to be able to master. Get the basics right and you will have a lifetime of enjoyment from your harmonica.

LESSON 10
Strike up the band...

As in the first book, this last section isn't a lesson...it's your jam session!

All the **FastTrack®** books (Guitar, Keyboard, Bass, Drums, Singer, and Saxophone) have the same last section. This way, you can either play by yourself along with the audio, or form a band with your friends.

We're also going to continue using harps in different keys, but as long as you grab the right harp and follow the tablature symbols, you'll be all set to play along.

So, whether the band is on the audio or in your garage, let the show begin...

SONG INDEX
(...gotta have one!)